MUNCHING ON CHURROS IN MEXICO

GEOGRAPHY LITERACY FOR KIDS | CHILDREN'S MEXICO BOOKS

Speedy Publishing LLC

40 E. Main St. #1156

Newark, DE 19711

www.speedypublishing.com

Copyright 2017

All Rights reserved. No part of this book may be reproduced or used in any way or form or by any means whether electronic or mechanical, this means that you cannot record or photocopy any material ideas or tips that are provided in this book.

In this book, we're going to talk about visiting the colorful country of **Mexico**. So, let's get right to it!

WHERE IS THE COUNTRY OF MEXICO?

The northern edge of Mexico shares a long border with the United States and is south of the United States. On the map, it looks something like a mermaid's tail. To its west is the Pacific Ocean and to its east is the Gulf of Mexico. The landmass of Mexico covers 758,450 square miles.

MAP OF MEXICO BORDER

There are over 120 million people living in Mexico and their official language is Spanish. Mexico's southern border connects to Central America and the countries of Belize and Guatemala.

WHAT ARE THE GEOGRAPHIC FEATURES OF MEXICO?

The geography of Mexico has many extremes. It has very tall mountains, which are part of the Sierra Madre range. Sierra Madre means "mother mountains." The part of the mountain range that is in the east is called the Sierra Madre Oriental and the part that is in the west is called the Sierra Madre Occidental.

SIERRA MADRE

SILVER

In between the two parts of the range there are smaller mountains in the Central Plateau. The Central Plateau has rich mineral deposits of silver as well as copper.

The "tail" of Mexico juts into the Gulf of Mexico. This piece of the land is called the Yucatán Peninsula. It is surrounded on three sides by the Gulf of Mexico and the Caribbean Sea. The tip of the western edge of the country of Cuba is directly across from the tip of the Yucatán Peninsula.

YUCATAN PENINSULA

The center of the country has mountainous regions and deep canyons. There are expansive deserts in the northern part of Mexico and the terrain changes to dense, humid rainforests in the southern regions and to the east.

Mexico has many rivers and lakes. The Colorado River and the Rio Grande River begin in the United States and continue in Mexico.

Mexico is a middle ground for animals escaping from the northern chill and the southern heat. The northern desert is home to many animals and plants that have learned to survive with very little water. The rainforests and wetlands are home to exotic species like quetzal birds, which the Mayans and Aztecs considered sacred.

WHAT IS THE CULTURE LIKE IN MEXICO?

Mexico has a rich heritage filled with great civilizations of native people. The Olmec people created the first of these civilizations. They were followed by the Mayan people, then the Toltec civilization, and then the Aztecs. All of these civilizations built amazing cities and had complex societies.

MAYAN PYRAMID

After the Spanish explorers came, they took over the country and ruled Mexico as their territory for three hundred years. Today, most of the people in Mexico come from a mixed heritage of Spanish and native ancestors.

Mexico has always been a center for amazing art and architecture. The early civilizations had step pyramids that rivaled the pyramids of Egypt. The native peoples made beautiful murals as well as detailed sculptures and elaborate jewelry. In Mexico, art is a way of life. Today there are master painters, muralists, and sculptors living and working in Mexico.

AZTEC SERPENT SCULPTURE

Sports have also been important in Mexico since their first civilizations. Some of the first sports involved shooting a ball through a stone hoop built above a plaza. The stakes were high since the losers were put to death. Today, there are still dangerous, life-risking sports, such as bullfighting. Rodeo, which was invented in Mexico, is another sport where competitors risk their lives.

WHAT PLACES ARE GOOD FOR EXPLORING IN MEXICO?

There are so many amazing places to visit in Mexico. You can relax on the beautiful sandy beaches. You can go exploring in the ruins of the ancient Aztec and Mayan cities or the historic Spanish colonial villages. Many of these locations are so important that they have been named UNESCO World Heritage Sites. Mexico has delicious food and vibrant music and dance traditions.

MAYAN CITY

Cancun and the Mayan Riviera

If you love the beach, you will want to visit the city of Cancún as well as Playa del Carmen and the beautiful island of Cozumel. These three locations have been named the "Mayan Riviera" and are located on the Yucatán Peninsula at the tip of the coastline. You can go swimming with dolphins or stingrays. You can go snorkeling among colorful tropical fish in between gorgeous coral reefs.

You can even go scuba diving to see the largest museum in the world that has underwater sculptures. A closeby drive will take you to the Mayan ruins of Chichén Itzá with its ritual ball courts and incredible architecture as well as Tulum, an ancient Mayan fort. Tulum's ancient stone ruins can be seen for miles away since they are on tall cliffs that face the crystal-clear Caribbean Sea.

Puerto Vallarta

Puerto Vallarta is a popular beach resort on the Pacific coastline of Mexico. People from all over North America began to come to the pristine beaches here in the 1960s. Many people from other countries have bought second homes here. If you want to try paragliding or jet skiing, you'll have plenty of opportunities in Puerto Vallarta.

The Aztec Pyramids

Some of the main attractions in Mexico are the Aztec pyramids. Unlike the Egyptian pyramids, the Aztecs designed pyramids that have a step pattern. The Aztecs built three types of pyramids.

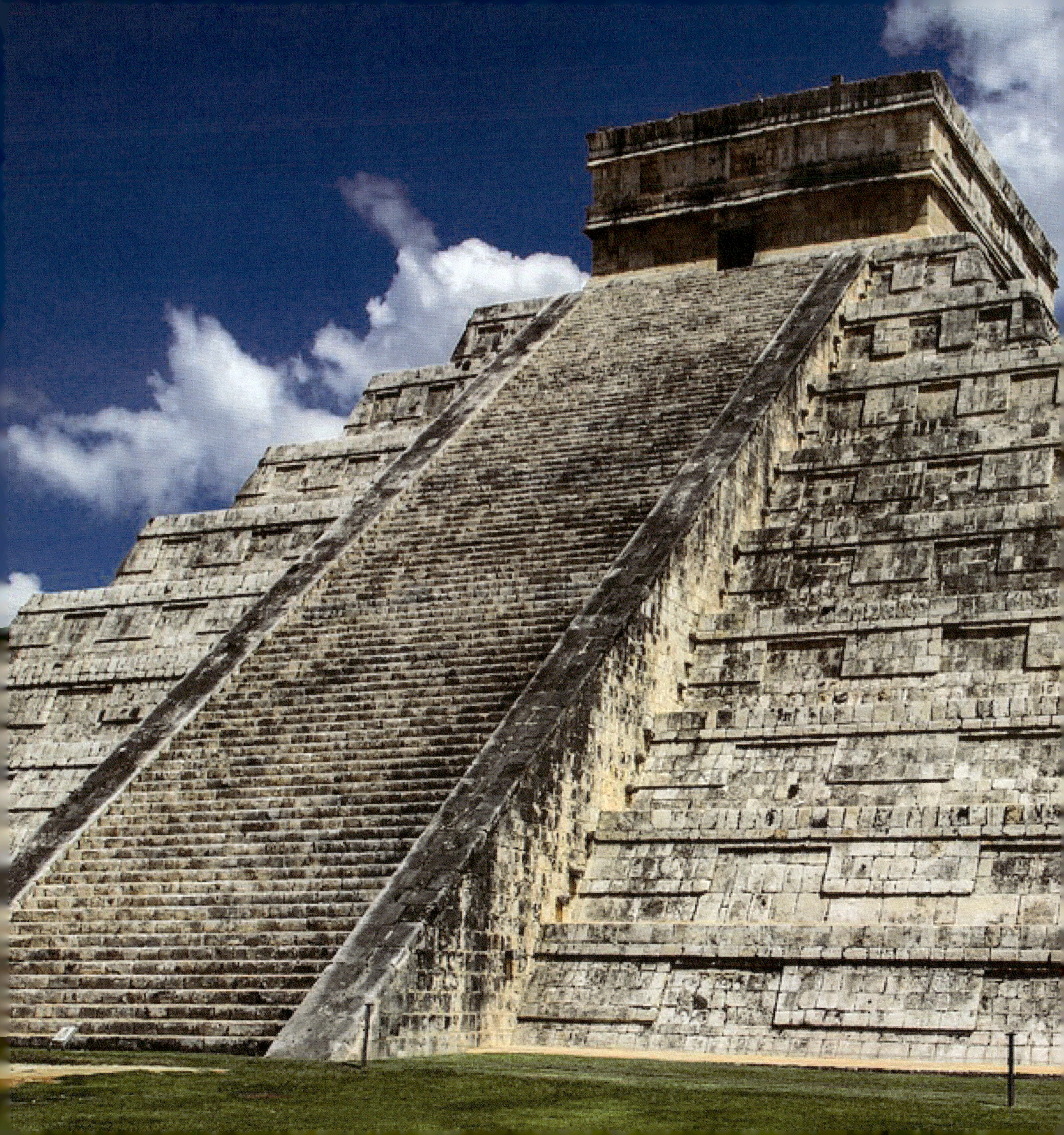

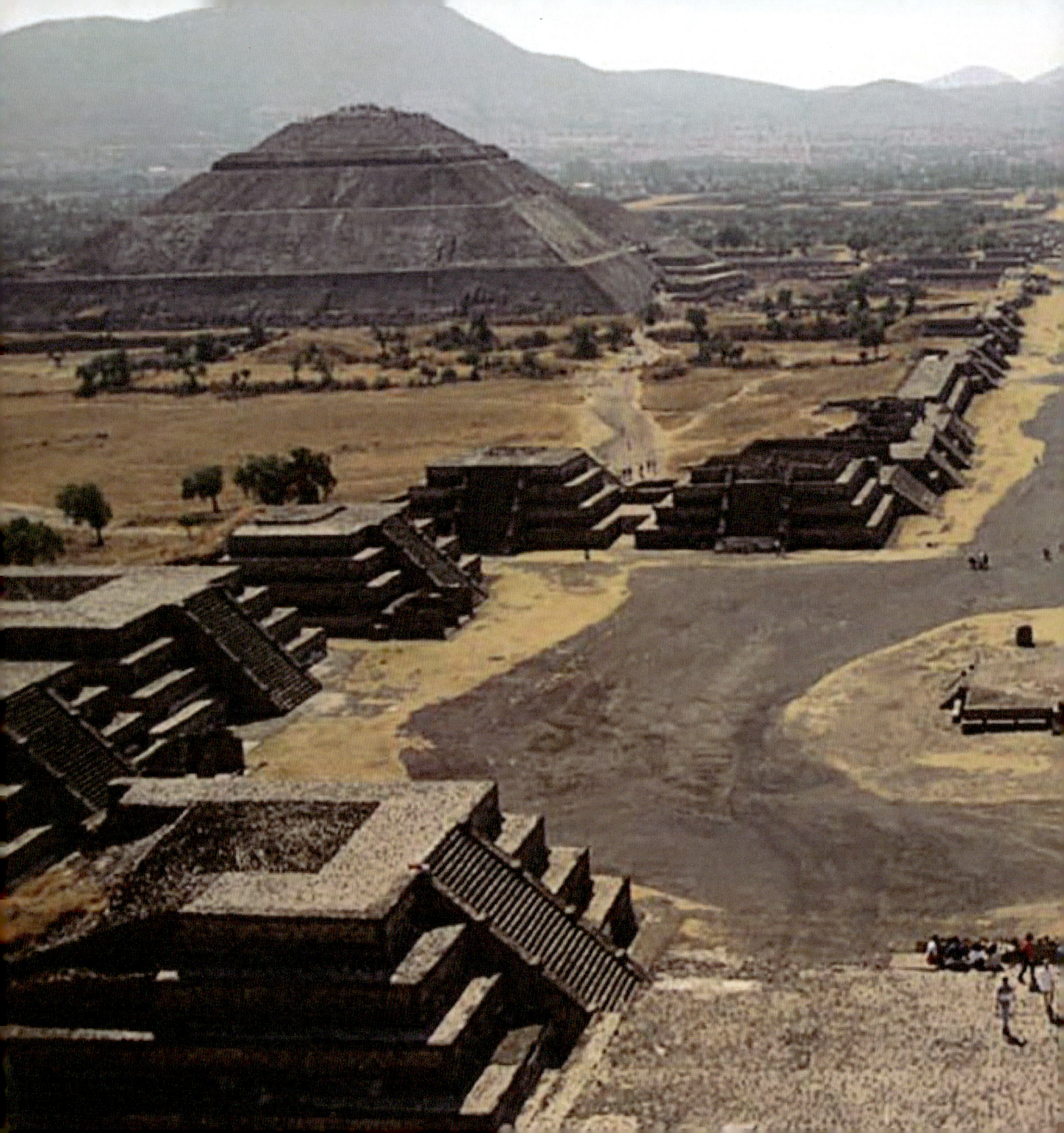

Twin-stair pyramids had double staircases. They also had two temples located at the very top. Each temple was dedicated to a different god. Twin-stair pyramids had bases that were square.

Pyramids that were built for the god Quetzalcoatl weren't as common. Some of these pyramids have a round base. Quetzalcoatl was the god of the wind.

They also built single-stair pyramids with square bases later in their civilization.

QUETZALCOATL

PYRAMID OF THE SUN

There are five parks where you can explore the Aztec ruins in Mexico. In many places you can climb to the top to see expansive views. Teotihuacan has two of the largest pyramid structures in the world—the Pyramid of the Sun and the Pyramid of the Moon. Surprisingly, the Aztecs didn't build these pyramids. They found the abandoned city in the 13th century. Archaeologists believe these pyramids were built by another civilization at least one thousand years before the Aztecs.

Mexico City

The capital of Mexico is Mexico City and it is one of the largest cities in the world. The modern city was built on top of the ancient Aztec city of Tenochtitlan, which was constructed at the center of Lake Texcoco. The lake and the ruins are buried under the city. However, in 1978, archaeologists discovered the ruins of an ancient Aztec temple that is known today as Templo Mayor.

TEMPLO MAYOR

POPOCATÉPETL AND IZTACCIHUATL

Next to the ruins there is a museum that has artifacts that have been found there. In the center of the city is a historic area that has beautiful colonial buildings that the Spanish built from the 16th through the 19th centuries. There are two enormous volcanoes that are visible from the city—Popocatépetl, which is still active, and its companion Iztaccihuatl.

THE DAY OF THE DEAD

This unusual festival in Mexico is celebrated on November 1st and 2nd. It combines the ancient traditions of the Aztecs, which paid homage their dead ancestors, with the Catholic traditions of "All Souls' Day" that the Spanish brought with them from Europe in the 1500s. Most people think of skeletons as scary, but during the Day of the Dead, the skeletons are everywhere and they are colorful and joyful.

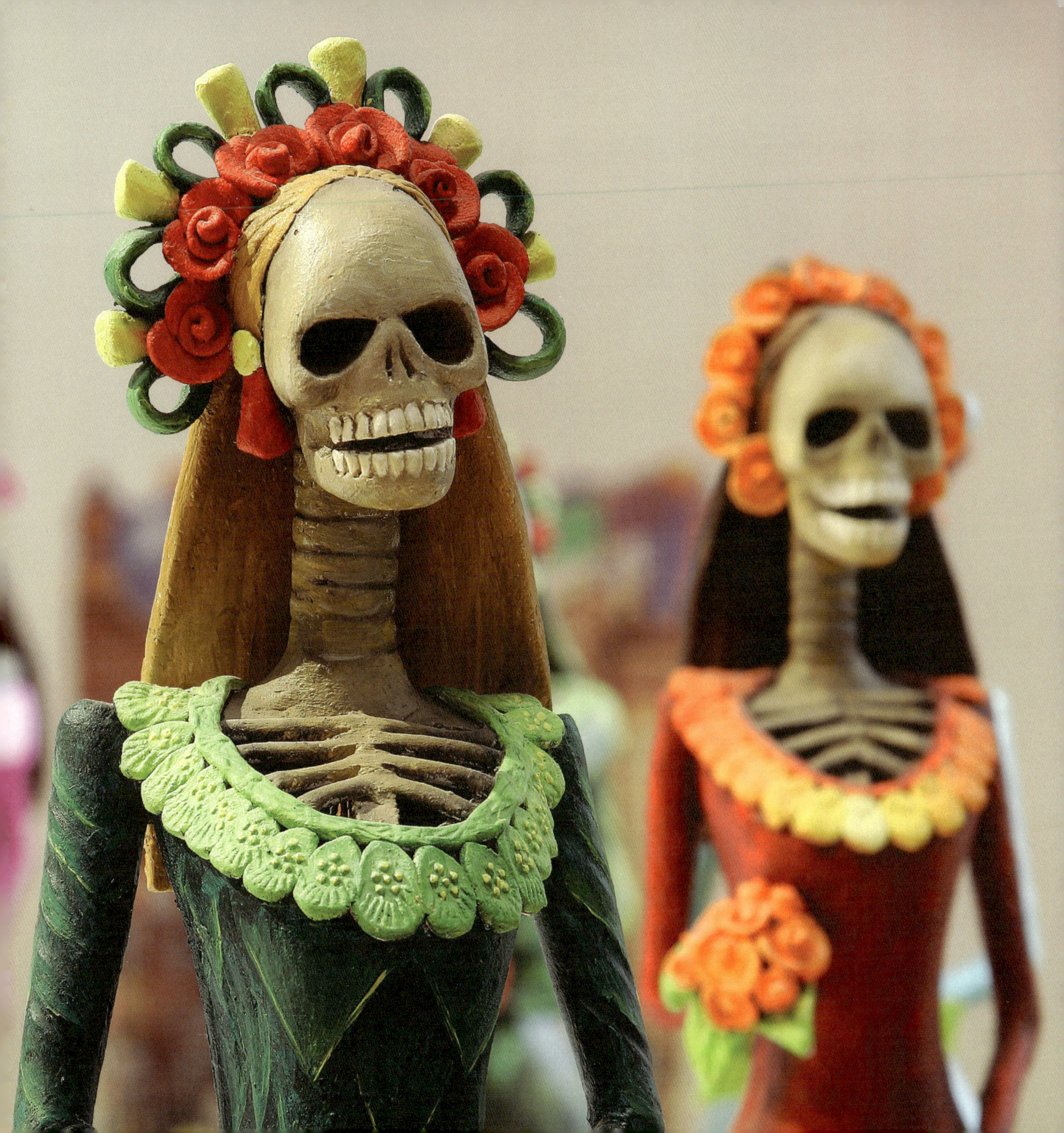

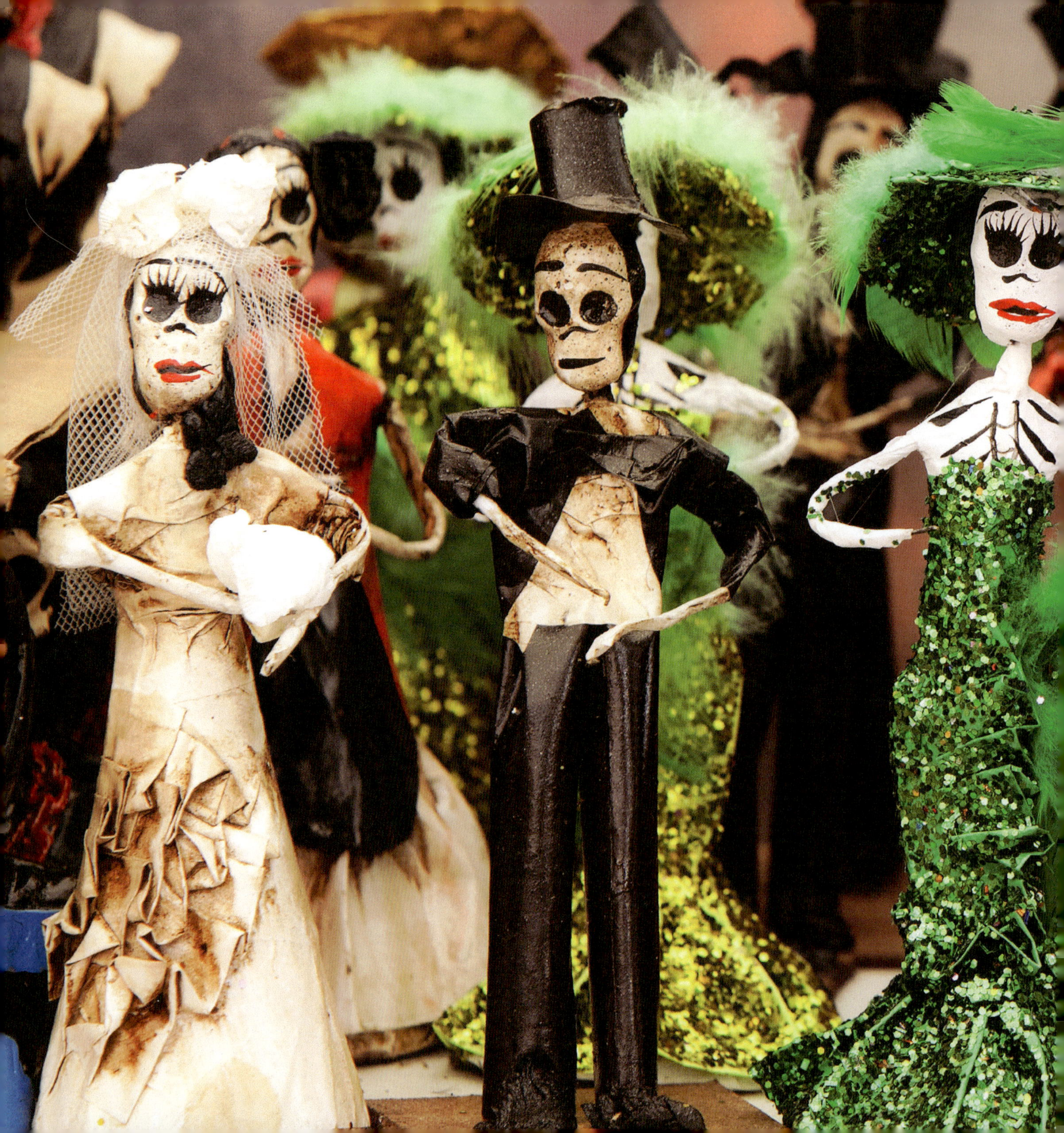

In addition to honoring the dead, this festival serves as a reminder to the living to enjoy life to the fullest before it's over! Traditional mariachi music is played and people dance into the night.

WHICH FOODS ARE FUN TO TRY IN MEXICO?

The streets in Mexico have hundreds of carts and stalls that have authentic specialties for you to try. Some are savory and some are sweet.

TACOS

FLAUTAS

Some of the favorite types of finger foods are called flautas. They are named after flutes because of their tube-like shape. They are huge, corn tortillas that are stuffed with pork or chicken or potatoes. Then, they are rolled, and deep-fried. When they dry out, they are crunchy, yummy snacks that can be dipped in sour cream before they're munched.

Churros are a favorite Mexican treat. They are crunchy pieces of fried dough that have cinnamon and sugar. Many street vendors at fairs in the United States serve their own version of churros.

CHURROS

PALACE OF FINE ARTS, MEXICO CITY

MEXICO HAS IT ALL!

Mexico has mountainous regions, an expansive desert, rainforests, and active volcanoes. Surrounded by the Pacific Ocean on its west and the Gulf of Mexico on its east, it has miles of beautiful coastline and beaches. The culture of Mexico is an interesting mixture of the native civilizations, such as the Mayans and Aztecs, combined with the European culture of the Spaniards. Mexico is filled with amazing art, ancient architecture, and delicious food.

Awesome! Now that you know more about the country of Mexico, you may want to find out more about the Aztec Civilization in the Baby Professor book **The Daily Life of an Aztec Family—History Books for Kids.**

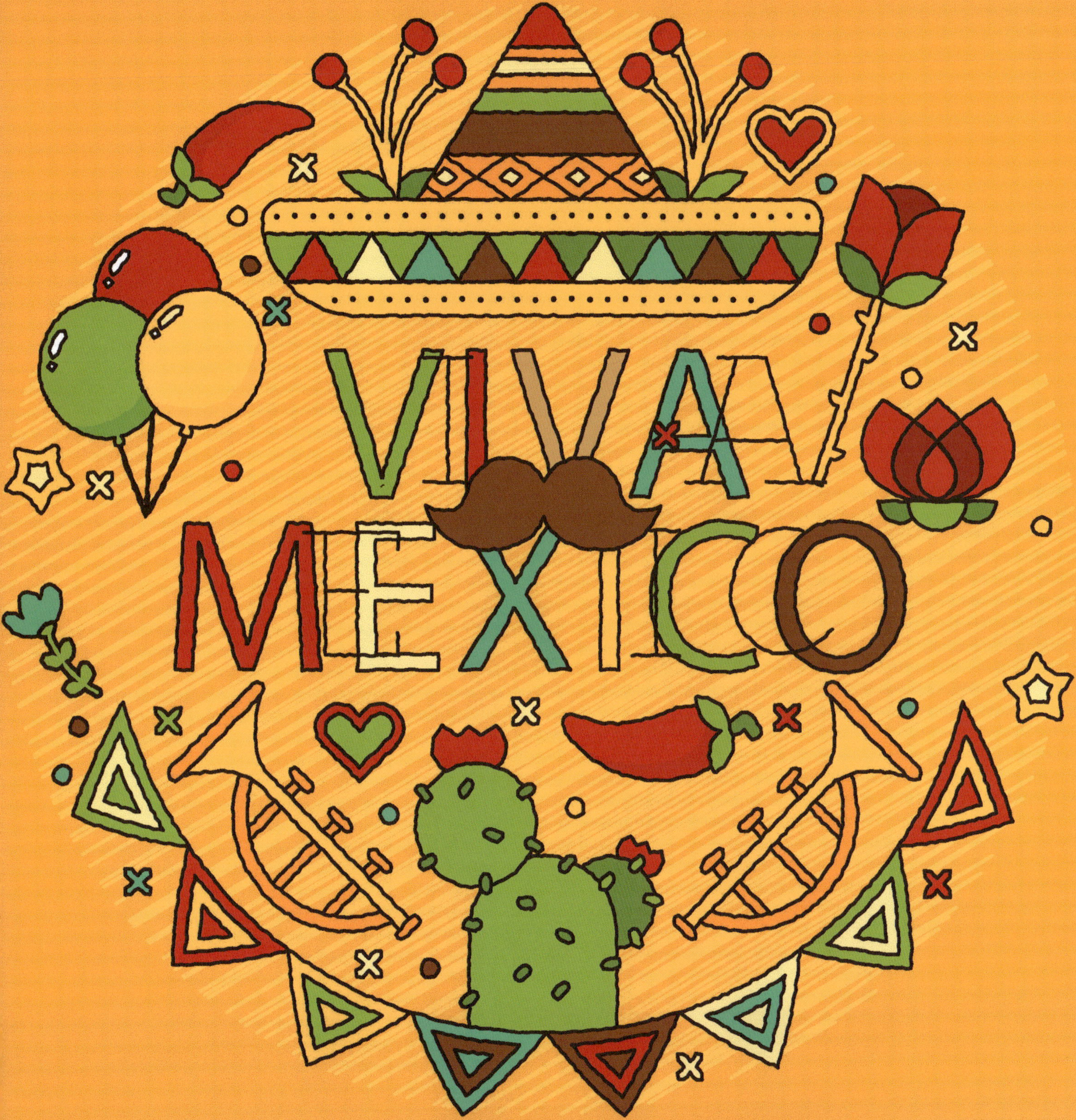
VIVA
MEXICO

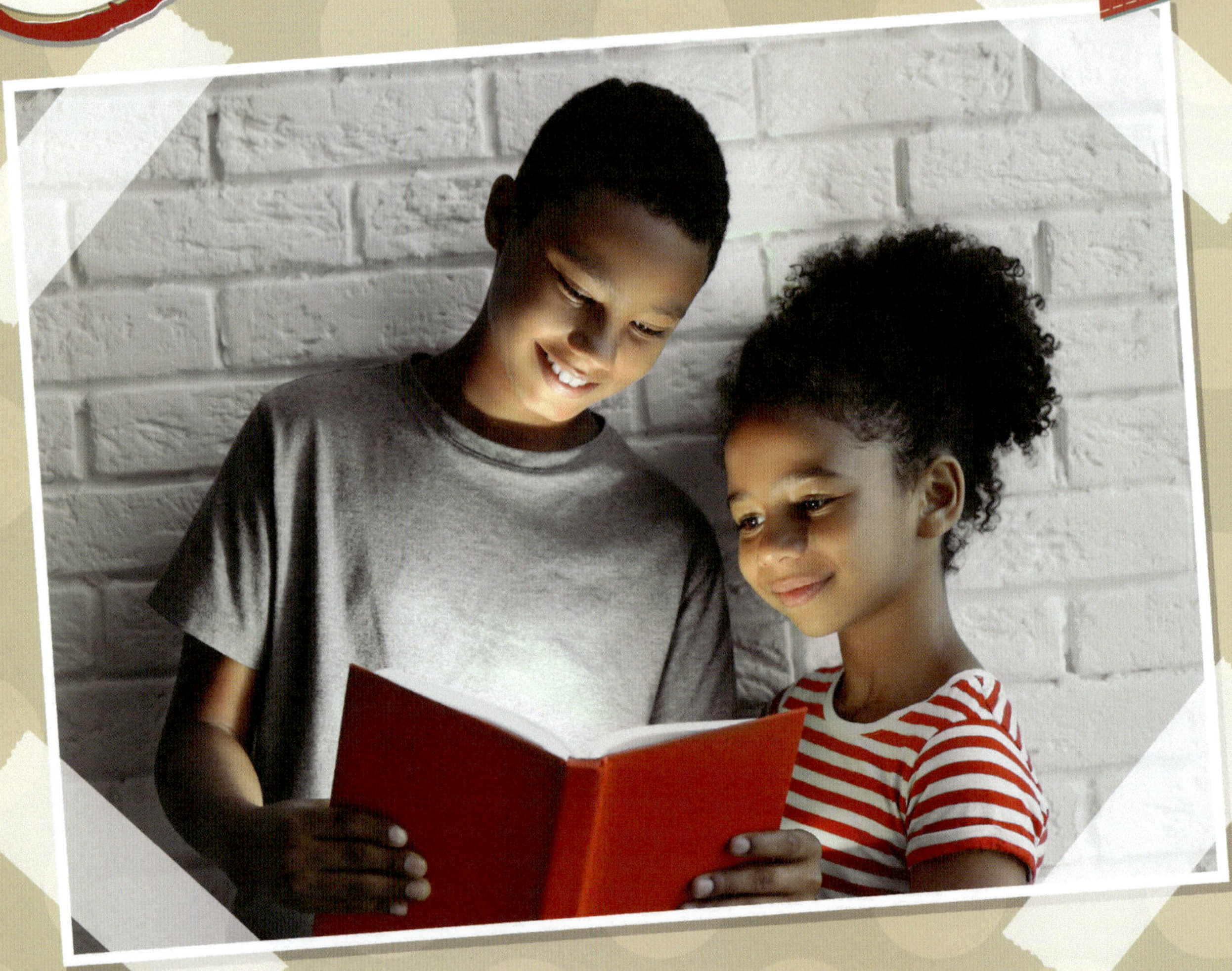

Visit

BABY PROFESSOR
EDUCATION KIDS

www.BabyProfessorBooks.com

to download Free Baby Professor eBooks and view our catalog of new and exciting Children's Books

46610430R00040

Printed in Poland
by Amazon Fulfillment
Poland Sp. z o.o., Wrocław